The Magic of Kindness
Copyright 2020 by Anita Mortley
All rights reserved. No part of this book may be used or reproduced in any manner whatsoever without written permission except in the case of brief quotations embodied in critical articles or reviews. Thank you for buying an authorized edition of this book and for complying with copyright laws by not reproducing, scanning, or distributing any part of it in any form without permission. You are supporting writers and their hard work by doing this.

For information contact:
Anita Mortley the.magicofkindness@yahoo.com

Written by Anita Mortley and illustrated by Aisha Vu
ISBN: 979-8-6796621-2-4
Library of Congress Cataloging-in-Publication Data is available Printed in the United States of America
First Edition: November 2020

This book is dedicated to my children Karei and Caiden Mortley. Mommy loves you.

Special thanks to

Cheryl Stamp, Benjamin, Willa and Kendall Sanford.
My wonderful parents, Lydia and David Canty.
My beautiful sister, Zalia Canty.
My amazing grandparents, Simeon and Marie Mortley.
The coolest uncle in the world, Sim Mortley.

The Magic of Kindness

By Anita Mortley

Illustrated by Aisha Vu

Available on Amazon   Instagram: the.magicofkindness

Ms. Sabra, a second grade teacher saw that her second grade friends were not being nice to each other. She called everyone to the rug and told her class.

I see a lot of children not being nice to each other and I know that we can do better.

She picks up a bracelet from her table and shows the class.

This is a kindness bracelet. I will be watching all of you to see which one of you is being kind.

Tomorrow, the student that I choose will wear the bracelet. At the end of the day he or she will choose the next kind student to wear the bracelet for the following day.

The next morning the class came to the rug for a morning meeting. She let them know that they've all been doing a great job.

Ms. Sabra announced that Akeem will get the bracelet for that day, because she saw that Akeem helped a friend put the puzzle pieces away at the end of indoor recess.

Akeem watched his friends all day so he could choose who to give the bracelet to at the end of the day.

He picked Ria, because she gave a sad friend a hug to help her feel better.

The next day Ria picked Nigel. Nigel picked Emily. Emily picked Abena. Abena picked Sira and Sira picked Jahir. It went on each day until each student got a chance to wear the bracelet once.

ONE DAY....

Akeem and his best friend Ria were walking home from school together as they do each day.

They saw a lot of people being mean to each other.

Then A light bulb went off for Akeem...

...and without saying anything to Ria he ran the rest of the way home.

Heeeeeeeey!
Ria shouted.

Ria ran after Akeem and caught up to him at his house. She was out of breath.

Why did you run off and leave me? Ria shouted

Sorry Akeem said

and was talking so fast with excitement.

Ria: Slow down and start over.

Akeem: Ria, remember the kindness bracelet Ms. Sabra has for our class?

Ria: Yes, I do Akeem; why do you ask?

Akeem: What if I made a machine that gave kindness to everyone in this town?

I would wear the sensor bracelet and it would light up whenever I am near people being unkind, and magically a machine will appear.

The machine will create a wind around them and make them stop and think about what they're doing.

Ria: Oh my gosh, that's a great idea.

How will you do it?

Akeem: Here is my plan...

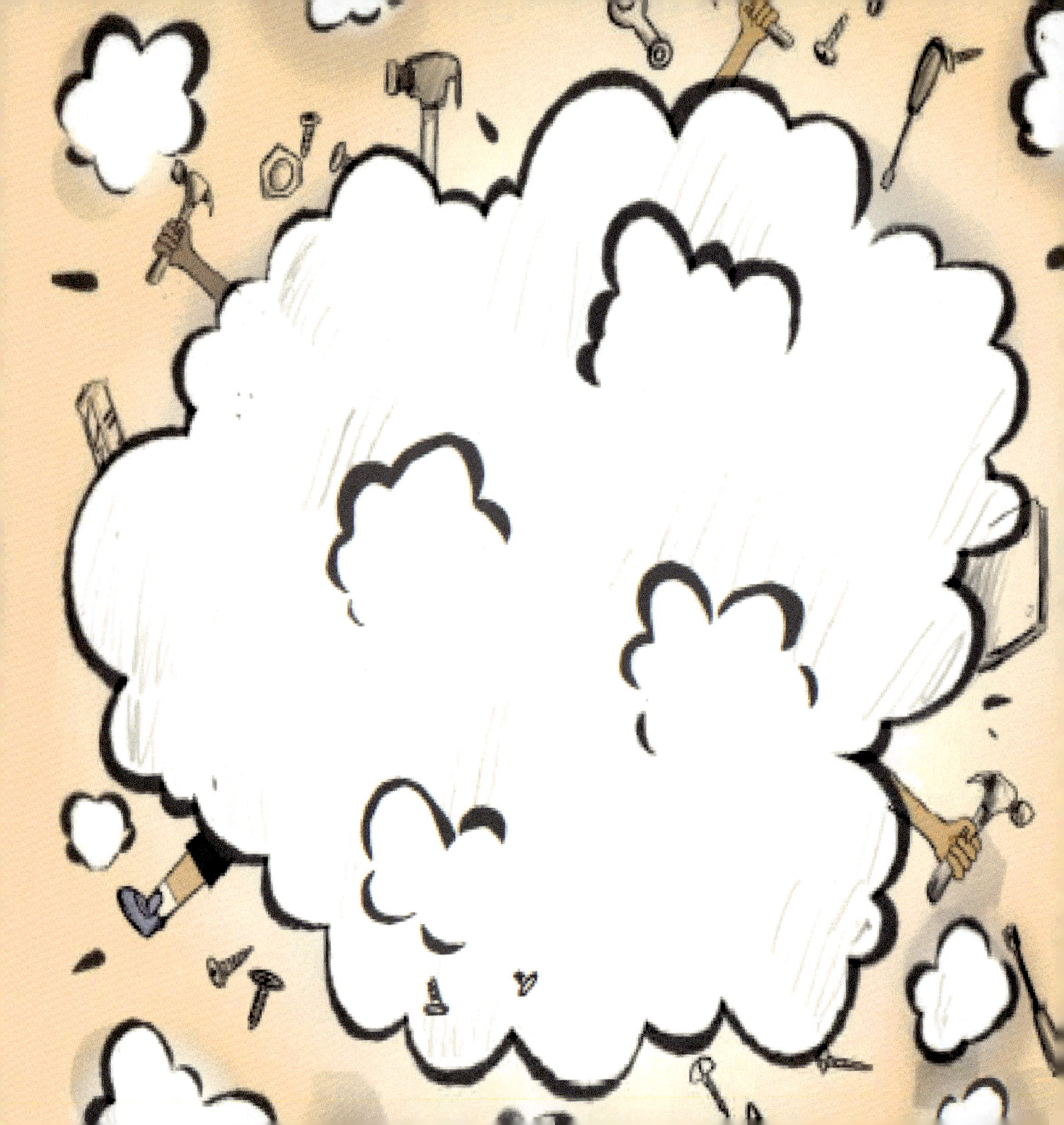

Two Weeks later!

Ria: Wow, this is amazing. You're going to help so many people change their mean ways.

Akeem wore the sensor bracelet the next day after school.

SCHOOL

As Akeem and Ria were walking home they kept looking around to see if people were being kind or not.

Ria: I'm so excited to see the machine work.

Akeem: Nooothing yet!

As they were about to pass the playground, Akeem's sensor bracelet lit up. Akeem and Ria looked around excitedly to see what the sensor bracelet found.

There was a kid yelling at another kid and saying mean things!

The machine appeared, and Akeem took off his bracelet and put it inside of his machine to give it the kindness touch.

A gust of wind blew over the older kid and he stopped and thought about what he was doing.

In a snap, the older kid, started to talk nicely with the younger kid.

Older Kid: I'm being mean, because I wanted to play with you and your friends. I don't have anyone to play with.

Younger Kid: We want to play with you too. All you had to do is ask.

Older Kid: I'm sorry.
Younger Kid: It's okay, let's play!

Ria: Wooow, Akeem. I can't believe it!!! The bracelet actually helped him to be kind!

Akeem: Yup, I told you it would work!

Day after day, Akeem was able to help people to be kind. Ms. Sabra couldn't have been more proud of what Akeem had made.

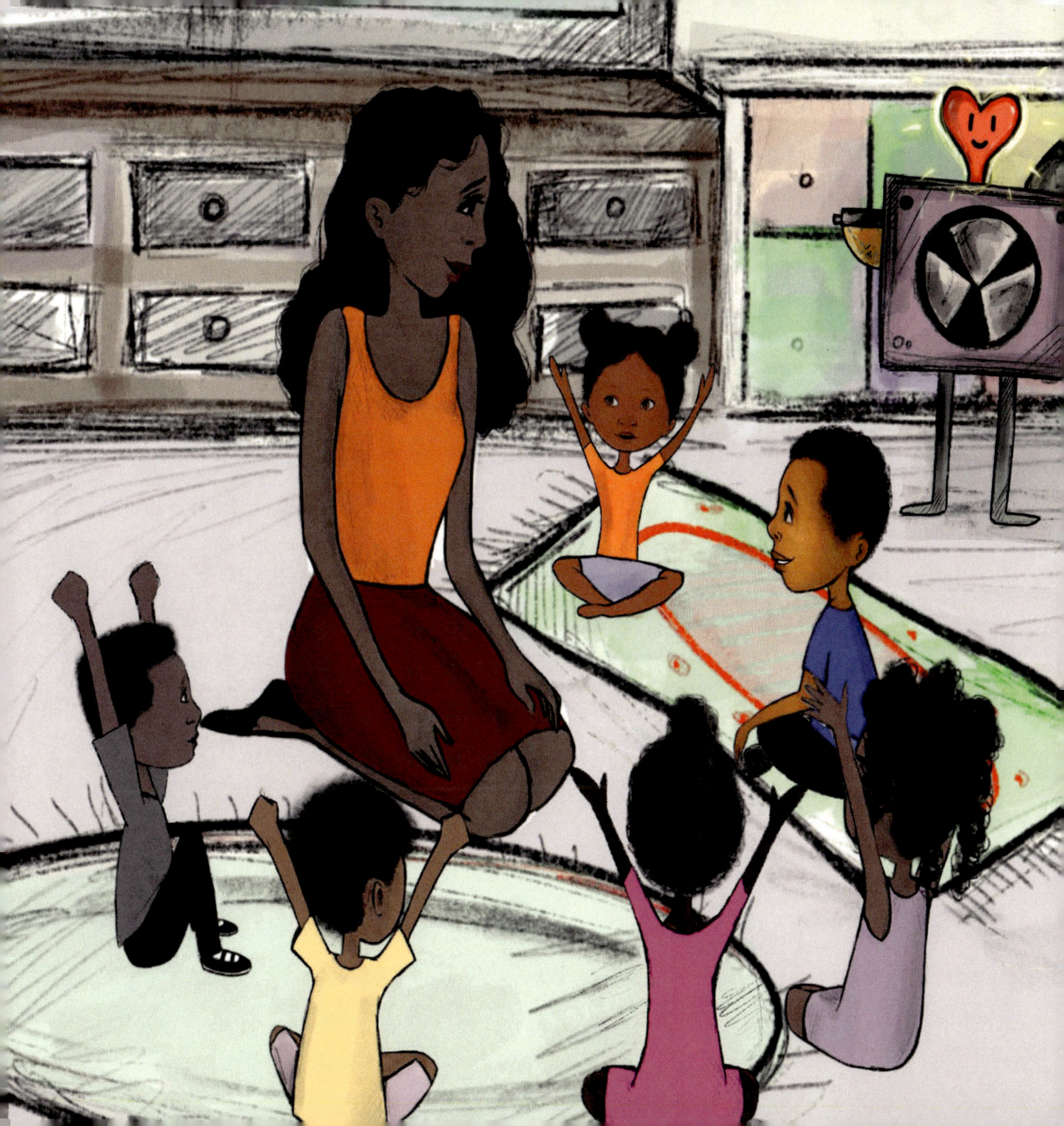

Anita Mortley is the mother of two boys, Karei and Caiden. She is a native of Brooklyn, New York, was raised in Boston, Massachusetts, and has a cultural background from the Caribbean island, Trinidad and Tobago.

Anita is a Social Psychology doctoral student; she currently works as a Behavioral Therapist and has been working with elementary students for three years. Her educational background in Psychology has given her a broad understanding of the way children's minds work. She especially enjoys seeing the positive behavioral differences as well as the intellectual growth of the students.

Photography by: Ari Williams
Instagram: @arilael

Reading Comprehension:

1. Who is the main character?

2. Why does the bracelet go into the machine?

3. What does the machine do?

I hope you enjoyed this book. Remember to be kind.

1. Akeem 2. The bracelet gives the machine the kindness touch. 3. The machine help kids to stop and think.

Made in the USA
Middletown, DE
14 August 2023

Glencoe/McGraw-Hill

A Division of The McGraw-Hill Companies

Copyright © by The McGraw-Hill Companies, Inc. All rights reserved.
Printed in the United States of America. Permission is granted to reproduce the material contained herein on the condition that such material be reproduced only for classroom use; be provided to students, teachers, and families without charge; and be used solely in conjunction with Glencoe products. Any other reproduction, for use or sale, is prohibited without prior written permission of the publisher.

Send all inquiries to:
Glencoe/McGraw-Hill
8787 Orion Place
Columbus, OH 43240-4027

ISBN: 0-07-823625-8　　　　　　　　　　　Diagnostic and Placement Tests

1 2 3 4 5 6 7 8 9 10　024　09 08 07 06 05 04 03 02 01 00

Glencoe Mathematics
Diagnostic and Placement Tests

Glencoe McGraw-Hill

New York, New York   Columbus, Ohio   Woodland Hills, California   Peoria, Illinois

Contents

Using Glencoe's Diagnostic and Placement Tests **2**
Placement Options **4**
When to Use the Placement Tests **5**
Interpreting Scores **8**
Scoring Guide Masters **10**
Using Placement Tests for Diagnostic Purposes **15**
Learning Objectives Masters **16**
Diagnostic Charts and Intervention Materials **20**
Diagnostic and Placement Test Masters **28**
Answer Keys **54**

Using Glencoe's *Diagnostic and Placement Tests*

This booklet is designed to be used in two ways.

- The four tests in this booklet provide tools for helping you make placement decisions within Glencoe's middle school and algebra series:

    Mathematics: Applications and Connections, Course 1 (MAC 1)
    Mathematics: Applications and Connections, Course 2 (MAC 2)
    Mathematics: Applications and Connections, Course 3 (MAC 3)
    Pre-Algebra: An Integrated Transition to Algebra & Geometry
    Algebra 1: Integration, Applications, Connections
    Algebra 1: Volumes One and Two (Algebra 1 in Two Years)
    Algebra: Concepts and Applications

    The tests are keyed to *Pathways for Success*, which contains the Glencoe Mathematics Grades 6–12 Scope and Sequence and the Pathways Through the Series chart.

- These tests also provide valuable diagnostic information. See pages 15–27 in this booklet for further information on using these tests as diagnostic tools.

Placement Decisions

In making placement decisions for a student, consider a variety of evidence, such as the student's mathematics grades, classroom observations, teacher recommendations, portfolios of student work, standardized test scores, and placement test scores. Use the results of these placement tests <u>in conjunction with other assessments</u> to determine which mathematics course best fits a student's abilities and needs.

Test Content

These placement tests measure ability, but they are *not* achievement tests. They cover prerequisite concepts, not every concept found in a Glencoe mathematics textbook.

As the *Pathways for Success* scope and sequence indicates, concepts are introduced, developed, and reinforced in consecutive courses. These placement tests measure student mastery of concepts and skills that have been introduced or developed in the student's current mathematics course, that are further developed in the next course, but that *are not* developed in the following course.

For example, consider the concept of *ordering decimals*, part of the Number Strand, in *Mathematics: Applications and Connections,* Courses 1–3. The concept is developed in Course 1, further developed in Course 2, but it is only reinforced in Course 3. If students have mastered ordering decimals, Course 3 might be appropriate for them, but if they have not, Course 2 would better meet their needs.

Some concepts are not included in these placement tests, because they are not critical to success in algebra, for example, combinations, probability, and triangle classification.

Some algebra and pre-algebra concepts are not included, because Glencoe continues the development of these essential concepts in each course.

> For example, in the Patterns and Functions Strand, the concept of *graphing linear functions* is introduced and developed in *Mathematics: Applications and Connections, Course 3, Pre-Algebra, Algebra: Concepts and Applications,* and *Algebra 1*. Therefore, it is not included in the placement tests.

The concepts included in each test correspond to the Glencoe *Pathways for Success* scope and sequence. Lists of Learning Objectives for each test item are found on pages 16–19 of this booklet.

Course Offerings and District Philosophy

In addition to student ability, district policy is a major factor in determining which courses a student takes. For example, your district may choose to offer either *Mathematics: Applications and Connections,* Course 3, or *Pre-Algebra*. These two courses require roughly equivalent ability levels. Both are designed to prepare students for success in *Algebra 1;* however, *Pre-Algebra,* as the title implies, contains more algebra content.

Algebra 1 and *Algebra 1: Volumes One and Two* (Algebra 1 in Two Years) are designed for different learning situations. The content is the same; however, the pacing is different. District policy may determine which of these courses is offered.

On the other hand, *Algebra 1* and *Algebra: Concepts and Applications* do *not* require equivalent ability levels, although they both provide a complete first year algebra course. The chart on page 7 compares these two algebra courses.

Placement Options

Each of the four placement tests helps you determine student placement in one of *two* Glencoe courses. The chart below summarizes the placement options for each test.

Current Course — now being taken or recently completed
Next Course — typically taken after the Current Course
Following Course — typically taken after the Next Course

Placement Options

Current Course	Placement Test	Next Course	Following Course
Grade 5	1	MAC 1	MAC 2
MAC 1	2	MAC 2	MAC 3 or Pre-Algebra
MAC 2	3	MAC 3 or Pre-Algebra	Algebra 1 or Algebra 1, Volumes One and Two

		Algebra for Lower-Achieving Students	Standard Algebra
MAC 3 or Pre-Algebra	4	Algebra: Concepts and Applications	Algebra 1 or Algebra 1, Volumes One and Two

MAC 1 = *Mathematics: Applications and Connections, Course 1*
MAC 2 = *Mathematics: Applications and Connections, Course 2*
MAC 3 = *Mathematics: Applications and Connections, Course 3*

When to Use the Placement Tests

In most situations, these placement tests are given near the end of the *Current Course*, in order to help determine student placement for the following year. You can also use these tests in special situations, such as a student transferring into your school mid-year or entering middle school with advanced mathematics ability.

Placement Tests Format

Placement Tests 1, 2, and 3 all use the same format. Each contains 30 multiple-choice questions and is divided into three parts. Part 1 tests prerequisite concepts. Part 2 provides exercises involving computation and basic applications. Part 3 requires students to use higher-level thinking skills.

Format of Placement Tests 1, 2, and 3 and General Placement Suggestions

	Description	Students with low scores . . .	Students with high scores . . .
Part 1	Concepts essential for the **Next Course**; prerequisites	will likely need intervention or remediation in the **Next Course**.	may be ready to take the **Next Course** or the **Following Course**.
Part 2	Concepts developed in the **Next Course**, but *not* developed in the **Following Course**	will likely do better in the **Next Course**.	may be ready to take the **Following Course**.
Part 3	Same concepts as Part 2, involving higher-level thinking skills	will likely do better in the **Next Course**; will likely find the **Following Course** too challenging.	are ready to take the **Following Course**.

© Glencoe/McGraw-Hill   Diagnostic and Placement Tests

Placement Test 4 helps determine placement between *Algebra: Concepts and Applications* and *Algebra 1*. This test has a slightly different format. Its 32 multiple-choice questions are grouped into 4 parts.

The four parts differ in content, in learning style, and in thinking level, as shown in the chart below.

Format of Placement Test 4 and General Placement Suggestions

	Description	Thinking and learning styles	Students with high scores...	Students with low scores...
Part 1	Basic middle-school number concepts—proportional reasoning, distributive property, and property of proportions	logical	will likely need intervention or remediation in *Algebra: Concepts and Applications*.	may be ready for either *Algebra: Concepts and Applications* or *Algebra 1*.
Part 2	Concrete representations of basic pre-algebra concepts—adding integers with a number line, solving equations with models, and simplifying polynomials with algebra tiles	concrete thinking, visual/spatial and kinesthetic	will likely do better in *Algebra: Concepts and Applications*.	may be ready for either *Algebra: Concepts and Applications* or *Algebra 1*.
Part 3	Pre-algebra concepts in symbolic form	abstract thinking, logical	will likely do better in *Algebra: Concepts and Applications*.	are ready for *Algebra 1*.
Part 4	Two-step word problems, exponents, integers, expressions, equations, and basic coordinate graphs	abstract thinking, verbal/linguistic, logical	will likely do better in *Algebra: Concepts and Applications*.	are ready for *Algebra 1*.

© Glencoe/McGraw-Hill   Diagnostic and Placement Tests

Placement Test 4 Comparison Chart
Algebra: Concepts and Applications and Algebra 1

Placement Test 4

	Number of questions	Content
Part 1 (1–6)	6	Basic number concepts using fractions and decimals
Part 2 (7–12)	6	Pre-algebra concepts using concrete and graphic models
Part 3 (13–22)	10	Pre-algebra concepts using symbols and mathematical vocabulary
Part 4 (23–32)	10	Two-step verbal problems, basic algebra and function concepts, graphs

Course Comparisons

Algebra: Concepts and Applications	*Algebra 1*
Number concepts are further developed. Prerequisite skills are addressed. Subskills are reviewed where used, in Getting Ready.	Number concepts are reinforced, but not developed.
Models are used extensively. Hands-On Algebra activities help students move from concrete to abstract thinking. Info-Graphics present concepts visually.	Models are used to introduce topics, but students soon move on to symbolic representations.
Important concepts are described with words, numbers, and symbols. Exercises closely follow the Examples and provide plenty of practice.	Symbolic representations are emphasized, along with verbal, numerical, and graphic representations.
This course requires less reading. Reading Algebra features provide extra help. Vocabulary is emphasized. Critical Thinking exercises help students develop thinking skills.	Students are expected to read fairly well. Critical Thinking exercises require students to explain and justify. Math Journal activities strengthen communication skills.

© Glencoe/McGraw-Hill   Diagnostic and Placement Tests

Interpreting Scores

When you interpret scores on the placement tests, consider the student's score on each part, as well as the total score. Scoring Guide Masters on pages 10–13 can be reproduced and used to record each student's score. A sample of a completed Scoring Guide for Test 1 is shown below; a sample for Test 4 is provided on the next page.

The shaded boxes show the range of scores that corresponds to each placement option. If a student's scores on each part of the test fall in the same shaded range, then that course is probably the best placement decision. If a student's scores fall in different ranges or near range boundaries, then analyze the results for each part and use additional assessment results to help determine placement.

Sample Score and Placement Analysis

Sample Score: On Placement Test 1, this student scored 5 questions correct in Part 1, 10 in Part 2, and 5 in Part 3. The total number correct was 20 out of 30.

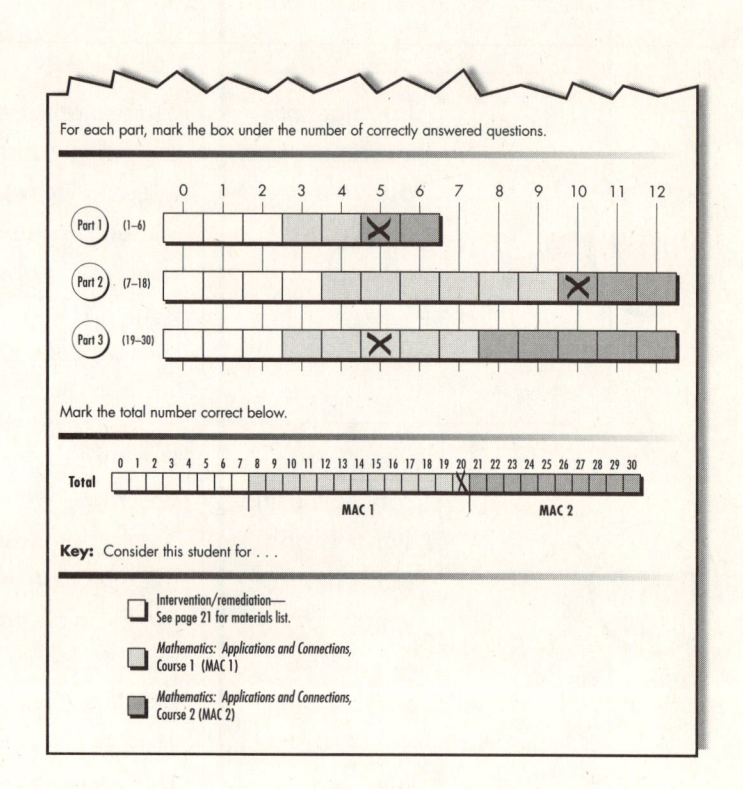

Sample Analysis

This student scored high on Part 1 and Part 2, but scored in the middle range on Part 3, which tests higher-level thinking skills. If these results are similar to other assessments, this student is likely to do well in *Mathematics: Applications and Connections,* Course 1, but will likely find *Mathematics: Applications and Connections,* Course 2, too challenging.

© Glencoe/McGraw-Hill   Diagnostic and Placement Tests

Scoring Placement Test 4

The Scoring Guide for Test 4 is slightly different. It includes four parts, rather than three.

Students who score in the *Algebra 1* range for each of the four parts are ready for *Algebra 1*. Students who score in the *Algebra: Concepts and Applications* range or below in each of the four parts, are best served by *Algebra: Concepts and Applications*.

To place students who score in the *Algebra 1* range on only two or three parts, use other factors, such as previous mathematics grades and teacher recommendations.

Sample Score and Placement Analysis

Sample Score: On Placement Test 4, this student scored 6 questions correct in Part 1, 5 in Part 2, 7 in Part 3, and 5 in Part 4. The total number correct was 23 out of 32.

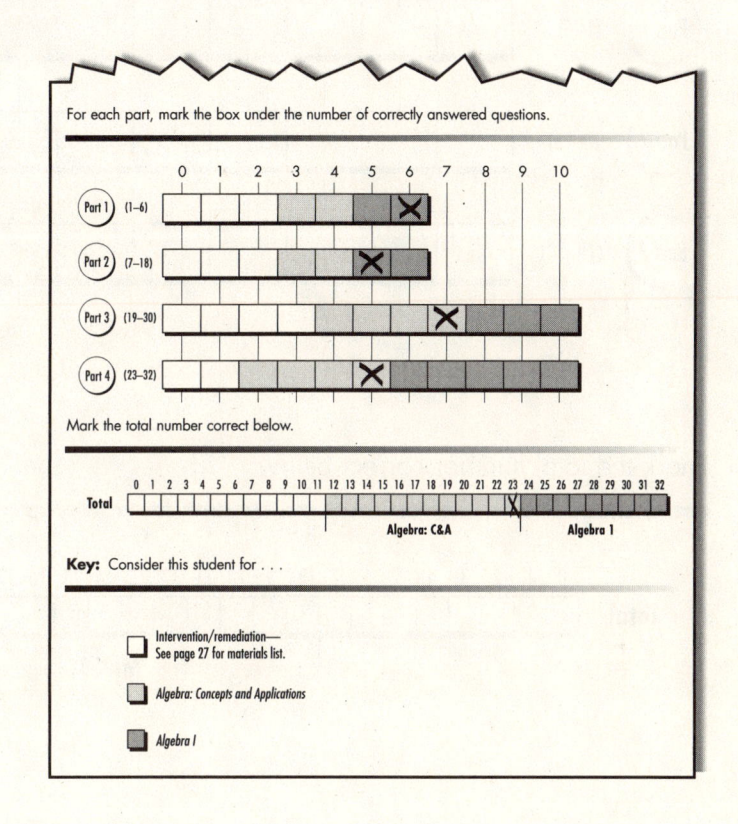

Sample Analysis

This student could be placed in either algebra course. This student will likely do well in *Algebra: Concepts and Applications,* but many find *Algebra 1* challenging. This student may need additional help to succeed in *Algebra 1* since Parts 3 and 4 show relatively low scores. Check which questions were missed to determine whether the student has English language or reading difficulties.

Placement Test 1
Scoring Guide

Student Name _____

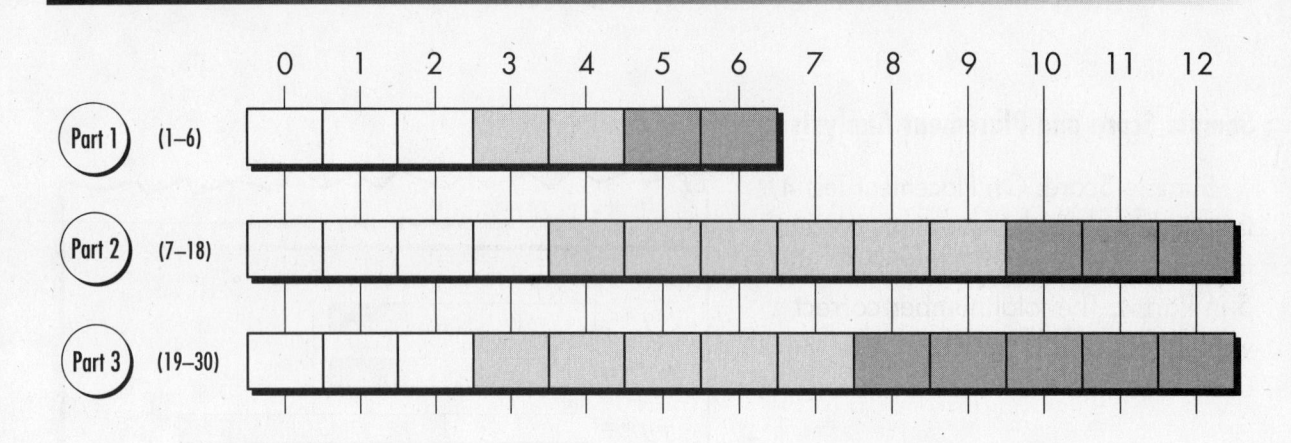

For each part, mark the box under the number of correctly answered questions.

		0	1	2	3	4	5	6	7	8	9	10	11	12
Part 1	(1–6)													
Part 2	(7–18)													
Part 3	(19–30)													

Mark the total number correct below.

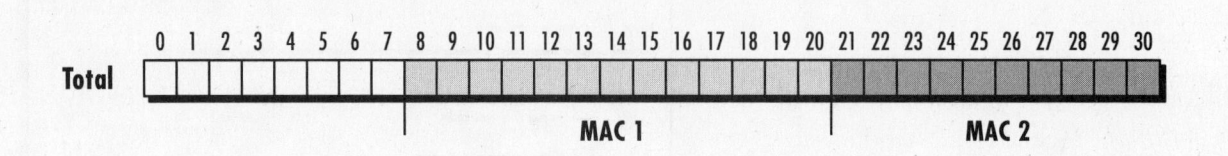

Total: 0 1 2 3 4 5 6 7 | 8 9 10 11 12 13 14 15 16 17 18 19 20 | 21 22 23 24 25 26 27 28 29 30

                          MAC 1   MAC 2

Key: Consider this student for . . .

- ☐ Intervention/remediation—
  See page 21 for materials list.

- ☐ *Mathematics: Applications and Connections,*
  Course 1 (MAC 1)

- ☐ *Mathematics: Applications and Connections,*
  Course 2 (MAC 2)

© Glencoe/McGraw-Hill   Diagnostic and Placement Tests

Placement Test 2 Scoring Guide

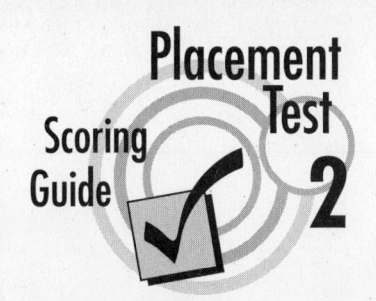

Student Name _____

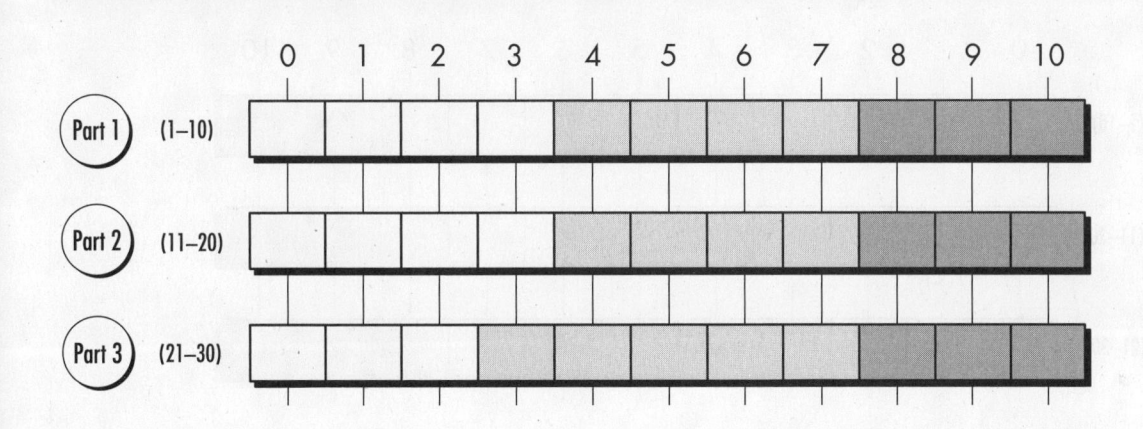

For each part, mark the box under the number of correctly answered questions.

	0	1	2	3	4	5	6	7	8	9	10
Part 1 (1–10)											
Part 2 (11–20)											
Part 3 (21–30)											

Mark the total number correct below.

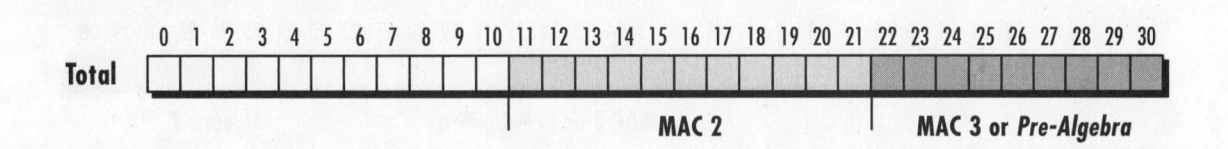

Total: 0 1 2 3 4 5 6 7 8 9 10 11 12 13 14 15 16 17 18 19 20 21 22 23 24 25 26 27 28 29 30

MAC 2 (11–21)   MAC 3 or *Pre-Algebra* (22–30)

Key: Consider this student for . . .

- ☐ Intervention/remediation—See page 23 for materials list.
- ☐ *Mathematics: Applications and Connections,* Course 2 (MAC 2)
- ☐ *Mathematics: Applications and Connections,* Course 3 (MAC 3) or *Pre-Algebra*

© Glencoe/McGraw-Hill   Diagnostic and Placement Tests

Placement Test 3 Scoring Guide

Student Name _____

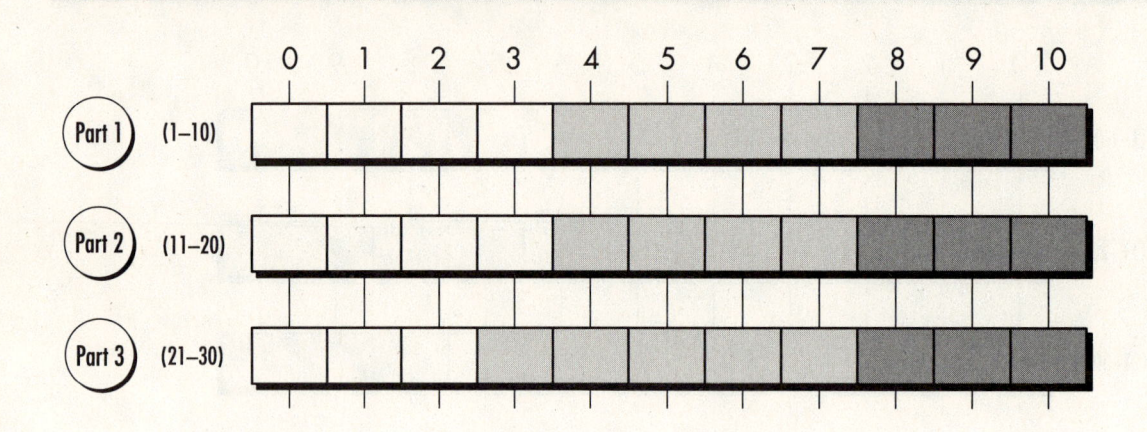

For each part, mark the box under the number of correctly answered questions.

```
           0   1   2   3   4   5   6   7   8   9   10
Part 1 (1–10)
Part 2 (11–20)
Part 3 (21–30)
```

Mark the total number correct below.

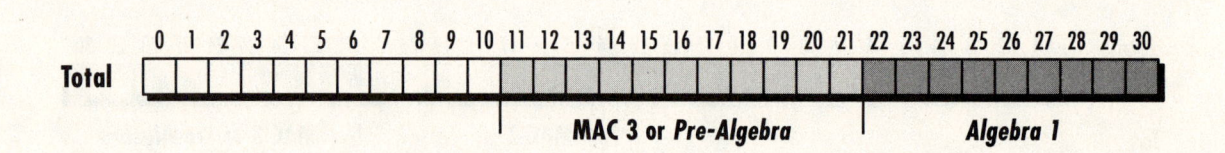

```
        0 1 2 3 4 5 6 7 8 9 10 11 12 13 14 15 16 17 18 19 20 21 22 23 24 25 26 27 28 29 30
Total
                              |  MAC 3 or Pre-Algebra   |        Algebra 1
```

Key: Consider this student for . . .

- ☐ Intervention/remediation—
  See page 25 for materials list.

- ☐ *Mathematics: Applications and Connections,*
  Course 3 (MAC 3) or *Pre-Algebra*

- ☐ *Algebra 1* or *Algebra 1,*
  Volumes One and Two

© Glencoe/McGraw-Hill — Diagnostic and Placement Tests

Placement Test 4 Scoring Guide

Student Name _____

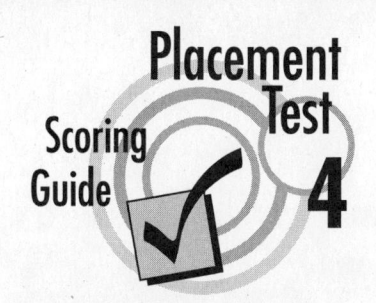

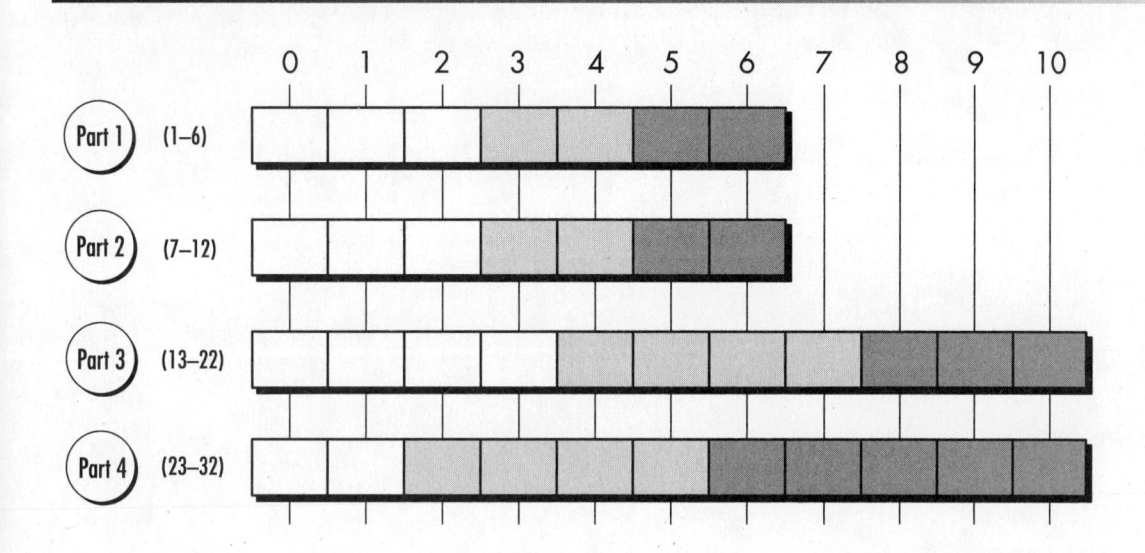

For each part, mark the box under the number of correctly answered questions.

		0	1	2	3	4	5	6	7	8	9	10
Part 1	(1–6)											
Part 2	(7–12)											
Part 3	(13–22)											
Part 4	(23–32)											

Mark the total number correct below.

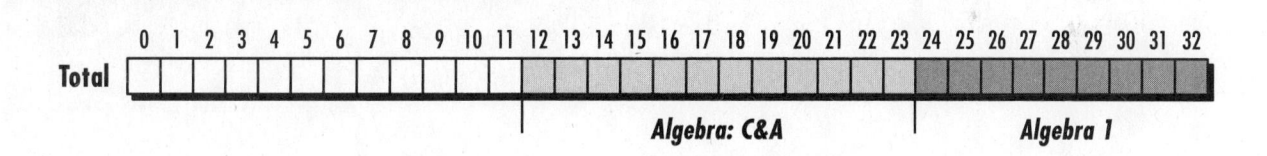

Total: 0 1 2 3 4 5 6 7 8 9 10 11 12 13 14 15 16 17 18 19 20 21 22 23 24 25 26 27 28 29 30 31 32

                                            Algebra: C&A   **Algebra 1**

Key: Consider this student for . . .

☐ Intervention/remediation—
See page 27 for materials list.

▨ *Algebra: Concepts and Applications*

▨ *Algebra 1*

© Glencoe/McGraw-Hill   Diagnostic and Placement Tests

Using Placement Tests for Diagnostic Purposes

These placement tests also provide valuable diagnostic information for classroom teachers. Reproducible learning objective charts, on pages 16–19, list the learning objective for each test question. By marking each question the student answered incorrectly, you can see which objectives the student has not mastered.

You can use the learning objective charts along with the *Pathways for Success* scope and sequence chart to find the page numbers in each textbook where an objective is introduced, developed, or reinforced.

Glencoe's wide variety of supplementary materials, such as Study Guide Masters, Practice Masters, and TestCheck and Worksheet Builder, can provide intervention and remedial help. Diagnostic charts for each test, on pages 20–27, describe the intervention that students may require and include a list of Glencoe print and technology materials.

If these tests are given near the end of the student's current course, it is recommended that the diagnostic information be shared with the teacher of that student's next course, in order to provide appropriate intervention during the next year.

Placement Test 1
Learning Objectives

Student Name _____

In the column on the left, mark the questions that the student answered *incorrectly*.

May Need Intervention	#	Strand	Objective

Part 1

May Need Intervention	#	Strand	Objective
☐	1	Number	order whole numbers
☐	2	Number	round whole numbers
☐	3	Number	add whole numbers with regrouping
☐	4	Number	subtract whole numbers with regrouping
☐	5	Number	word problem with whole numbers (multiplication, division)
☐	6	Number	word problem, 2-step (addition, subtraction)

Part 2

	#	Strand	Objective
☐	7	Number	subtract decimals
☐	8	Number	multiply decimal by whole number
☐	9	Number	simplify fractions
☐	10	Number	fractions, LCD
☐	11	Number	write a fraction with denominator of 10 or 100 as a decimal
☐	12	Number	write a decimal as a fraction
☐	13	Measurement	convert metric measures
☐	14	Geometry	area of a rectangle
☐	15	Number	ordering decimals
☐	16	Number	express fraction as a decimal
☐	17	Number	solve a word problem with decimals
☐	18	Number	solve a word problem with fractions

Part 3

	#	Strand	Objective
☐	19	Number	subtract decimals
☐	20	Number	multiply decimal by whole number
☐	21	Number	simplify fractions
☐	22	Number	fractions, LCD
☐	23	Number	write a fraction with denominator of 10 or 100 as a decimal
☐	24	Number	write a decimal as a fraction
☐	25	Measurement	convert metric measures
☐	26	Geometry	area of a rectangle
☐	27	Number	ordering decimals
☐	28	Number	express a fraction as a decimal
☐	29	Number	solve a word problem with decimals
☐	30	Number	solve a word problem with fractions

© Glencoe/McGraw-Hill — Diagnostic and Placement Tests

Placement Test 2 — Learning Objectives

Student Name _____

In the column on the left, mark the questions that the student answered *incorrectly*.

Part 1

May Need Intervention	#	Strand	Objective
☐	1	Number	subtract decimals
☐	2	Number	multiply decimal by whole number
☐	3	Number	simplify fractions
☐	4	Number	fractions, LCD
☐	5	Number	write a fraction with denominator of 10 or 100 as a decimal
☐	6	Number	write a decimal as a fraction
☐	7	Number	ordering decimals
☐	8	Number	express fraction as a decimal
☐	9	Number / Measurement	solve a word problem with decimals, time units
☐	10	Number	solve a word problem with fractions

Part 2

May Need Intervention	#	Strand	Objective
☐	11	Number	identify equivalent fractions
☐	12	Number	order fractions
☐	13	Number	order of operations
☐	14	Number	relating decimals, fractions, percents
☐	15	Number	powers of ten
☐	16	Number	associative, commutative properties
☐	17	Number	integer representations
☐	18	Algebra	evaluate expressions
☐	19	Geometry	perimeter
☐	20	Geometry	area of a triangle

Part 3

May Need Intervention	#	Strand	Objective
☐	21	Number	identify equivalent fractions
☐	22	Number	order fractions
☐	23	Number	order of operations
☐	24	Number	relating decimals, fractions, percents
☐	25	Number	powers of ten
☐	26	Number	associative, commutative properties
☐	27	Number	integer representations
☐	28	Algebra / Number	evaluate expressions, order of operations
☐	29	Geometry	perimeter
☐	30	Geometry / Algebra	area of a rhombus and trapezoid, evaluate expression

© Glencoe/McGraw-Hill — Diagnostic and Placement Tests

Placement Test 3 — Learning Objectives

Student Name _____

In the column on the left, mark the questions that the student answered *incorrectly*.

May Need Intervention	#	Strand	Objective
Part 1			
☐	1	Number	identify equivalent fractions
☐	2	Number	order fractions
☐	3	Number, Algebra	order of operations, evaluate expressions
☐	4	Number	relating decimals, fractions, percents
☐	5	Number	relating decimals, fractions, percents
☐	6	Number	powers of ten
☐	7	Number	associative, commutative properties
☐	8	Geometry	perimeter
☐	9	Geometry, Algebra	area of a triangle, evaluate expressions
☐	10	Geometry, Algebra	area of a rhombus and trapezoid, evaluate expressions
Part 2			
☐	11	Number	terminating and repeating decimals
☐	12	Number	distributive property, multiply fractions
☐	13	Number, Proportional Reasoning	property of proportions
☐	14	Number, Proportional Reasoning	add and subtract fractions
☐	15	Number, Proportional Reasoning	multiply and divide fractions and mixed numbers
☐	16	Number, Proportional Reasoning	relating ratio and rates
☐	17	Number, Proportional Reasoning	percent equation
☐	18	Patterns and Functions	informal arithmetic and geometric sequences
☐	19	Algebra	write expressions and equations
☐	20	Data Analysis	line graphs
Part 3			
☐	21	Number	terminating and repeating decimals
☐	22	Number, Algebra	distributive property, solve 2-step equations
☐	23	Number, Proportional Reasoning	multiply and divide fractions
☐	24	Number, Algebra	add and subtract integers, multiply and divide integers, solve 2-step equations
☐	25	Patterns and Functions	informal arithmetic and geometric sequences
☐	26	Algebra	write expressions and equations
☐	27	Algebra	positive integer exponents
☐	28	Geometry	graphing ordered pairs
☐	29	Data Analysis	stem-and-leaf plots, median
☐	30	Data Analysis	organize data in a table, line graphs

© Glencoe/McGraw-Hill — Diagnostic and Placement Tests

Placement Test 4 — Learning Objectives

Student Name _____

In the column on the left, mark the questions that the student answered *incorrectly*.

May Need Intervention	#	Strand	Objective
Part 1			
☐	1	Number-Proportional Reasoning	multiply, divide fractions
☐	2	Number-Proportional Reasoning	add and subtract fractions
☐	3	Number-Proportional Reasoning	terminating and repeating decimals
☐	4	Number-Proportional Reasoning	operate with mixed numbers
☐	5	Number	distributive property
☐	6	Number-Proportional Reasoning	property of proportions
Part 2			
☐	7	Number	add and subtract integers with models
☐	8	Algebra	solve equations with models
☐	9	Geometry	graphing ordered pairs
☐	10	Geometry / Algebra	area of a trapezoid, use a formula, evaluate expressions
☐	11	Algebra	simplify polynomials with models, combine like terms
☐	12	Geometry	area of a parallelogram
Part 3			
☐	13	Patterns and Functions, Number	informal arithmetic and geometric sequences, operations with integers
☐	14	Number	multiply and divide integers
☐	15	Number	add and subtract integers
☐	16	Number / Algebra	order of operations, evaluate expressions
☐	17	Number	scientific notation
☐	18	Number-Proportional Reasoning	ratio and rates
☐	19	Number-Proportional Reasoning	fractions and decimals as percents
☐	20	Number-Proportional Reasoning	percent equation, relating decimals
☐	21	Algebra	solve simple equations
☐	22	Patterns and Functions	function table
Part 4			
☐	23	Number	2-step word problem, add and subtract decimals
☐	24	Number	2-step word problem, multiply, divide decimals
☐	25	Algebra / Number	positive integer exponents, operations with rational numbers
☐	26	Number	read, write integers, order integers, inequalities
☐	27	Algebra	write expressions and equations
☐	28	Data Analysis	scatter plot, positive, negative, or no correlation
☐	29	Data Analysis / Patterns and Functions	line graph, sketch graphs from events
☐	30	Data Analysis	line graphs
☐	31	Coordinate Geometry	graphing ordered pairs, graphing lines
☐	32	Patterns and Functions / Algebra	represent functions and relations, solve equations with two variables

© Glencoe/McGraw-Hill — Diagnostic and Placement Tests

Placement Test 1 Diagnostic Chart

Placement Options:
Mathematics: Applications and Connections, Course 1
or
Mathematics: Applications and Connections, Course 2

	Content	Suggestions for Intervention/Remediation
Part 1	Operations with whole numbers; order whole numbers; solve word problems with whole numbers	These concepts are essential for success in *Mathematics: Applications and Connections*, Course 1. Students who score low in this part will benefit from intervention.
Part 2	Operations with decimals; simplify fractions; relating fractions and decimals; order decimals; solve word problems with decimals and fractions; area of a rectangle	These concepts continue to be developed in *Mathematics: Applications and Connections*, Course 1, but not in *Mathematics: Applications and Connections*, Course 2. Students who score low in this part may need additional reinforcement and practice with these concepts.
Part 3	Operations with decimals; simplify fractions; relating fractions and decimals; order decimals; solve word problems with decimals and fractions; area of a rectangle	These problems involve higher-level thinking skills. Students who score low in this part and are placed in *Mathematics: Applications and Connections*, Course 1, will likely *not* need intervention. Students who score low in this part, but are placed in *Mathematics: Applications and Connections*, Course 2, will likely need additional help.

Intervention/Remediation Materials

Mathematics: Applications and Connections, Course 1

Print Materials	
Study Guide Masters	A brief explanation, along with examples and exercises, for every lesson in the Student Edition.
Practice Masters	Additional practice for every lesson in the Student Edition.
Study Guide and Practice Masters	A consumable version of the Study Guide Masters and Practice Masters for each lesson. *Also available in Spanish.*
Transition Booklet	Helps identify students weak in certain prerequisite skills.
Basic Skills: Reinforcement and Practice	Transparencies and worksheets for 92 basic skills correlated to the Student Edition.
Parent and Student Study Guide Workbook	A review of every lesson that can be used by the parent and student. *Also available in Spanish.*
Spanish Study Guide and Assessment	Spanish translations of lesson objectives, Study Guide Masters, and free response Chapter Tests.

Technology Products	
MathPASS CD-ROM	Offers a complete, self-paced, easy-to-use interactive tutorial program.
TestCheck and Worksheet Builder	Networkable software includes a Worksheet Builder to make worksheets and tests, a Student Module to take tests on screen, and a Management System to keep student records.
MindJogger Videoquizzes	Chapter review provided in a game-show format. *Available in VHS and DVD.*
Vocabulary PuzzleMaker Software	Improves students' mathematics vocabulary using crossword puzzles, scrambles, and word searches.
Glencoe Internet Site	Visit **glencoe.com** and find Online Study Tools, including self-grading lesson-by-lesson reviews, standardized test practice, and vocabulary review.

Placement Test 2 Diagnostic Chart

Placement Options:
Mathematics: Applications and Connections, Course 2
or
Mathematics: Applications and Connections, Course 3
or
Pre-Algebra

Content	Suggestions for Intervention/Remediation
Part 1 — Operations with decimals; simplify fractions; relating fractions and decimals; order decimals; solve word problems with decimals and fractions	These concepts are essential for success in *Mathematics: Applications and Connections,* Course 2. Students who score low in this part will benefit from intervention.
Part 2 — Represent fractions, decimals, percents; order fractions; area of triangle; using formulas for perimeter; order of operations; represent integers; associative and commutative properties	These concepts continue to be developed in *Mathematics: Applications and Connections,* Course 2, but not in *Mathematics: Applications and Connections,* Course 3, or *Pre-Algebra.* Students who score low in this part may need additional reinforcement and practice with some of these concepts.
Part 3 — Represent fractions, decimals, percents; area of triangle and trapezoid using formulas; order of operations; represent integers	These problems involve higher-level thinking skills. Students who score low in this part and are placed in *Mathematics: Applications and Connections,* Course 2, will likely *not* need intervention. Students who score low in this part, but are placed in *Mathematics: Applications and Connections,* Course 3, will likely need additional help.

Intervention/Remediation Materials

Mathematics: Applications and Connections, Course 2

Print Materials	
Study Guide Masters	A brief explanation, along with examples and exercises, for every lesson in the Student Edition.
Practice Masters	Additional practice for every lesson in the Student Edition.
Study Guide and Practice Workbook	A consumable version of the Study Guide Masters and Practice Masters for each lesson. *Also available in Spanish.*
Transition Booklet	Helps identify students weak in certain prerequisite skills.
Parent and Student Study Guide Workbook	A review of every lesson that can be used by the parent and student. *Also available in Spanish.*
Spanish Study Guide and Assessment	Spanish translations of lesson objectives, Study Guide Masters, and free response Chapter Tests.

Technology Products	
MathPASS CD-ROM	Offers a complete, self-paced, easy-to-use interactive tutorial program.
TestCheck and Worksheet Builder	Networkable software includes a Worksheet Builder to make worksheets and tests, a Student Module to take tests on-screen, and a Management System to keep student records.
MindJogger Videoquizzes	Chapter review provided in a game-show format. *Available in VHS and DVD.*
Vocabulary PuzzleMaker Software	Improves students' mathematics vocabulary using crossword puzzles, scrambles, and word searches.
Glencoe Internet Site	Visit **glencoe.com** and find Online Study Tools, including self-grading lesson-by-lesson reviews, standardized test practice, and vocabulary review.

© Glencoe/McGraw-Hill   Diagnostic and Placement Tests

Placement Test 3 Diagnostic Chart

Placement Options:
Mathematics: Applications and Connections, Course 3
or
Pre-Algebra
or
Algebra 1
or
Algebra 1, Volumes One and Two

	Content	Suggestions for Intervention/Remediation
Part 1	Basic number concepts representing fractions and decimals; area of triangle and trapezoid using formulas	These concepts are essential for success in *Mathematics: Applications and Connections*, Course 3, or *Pre-Algebra*. Students who score low in this part will benefit from intervention.
Part 2	Operations with fractions; distributive property; percent equation; sequences; writing algebraic expressions; line graphs	These concepts continue to be developed in *Mathematics: Applications and Connections*, Course 3, or *Pre-Algebra*, but not in *Algebra 1*. Students who score low in this part may need additional reinforcement and practice with some of these concepts.
Part 3	Operations with fractions; operations with integers; solving 2-step equations; sequences; graphing ordered pairs; stem-and-leaf plots	These problems involve higher-level thinking skills. Students who score low in this part and are placed in *Mathematics: Applications and Connections*, Course 3, or *Pre-Algebra* will likely *not* need intervention. Students who score low in this part and are placed in *Algebra 1* will likely need additional help.

© Glencoe/McGraw-Hill

Intervention/Remediation Materials

Mathematics: Applications and Connections, Course 3
and
Pre-Algebra: An Integrated Transition to Algebra & Geometry

Print Materials	
Study Guide Masters	A brief explanation, along with examples and exercises, for every lesson in the Student Edition. *Also available as a workbook for Pre-Algebra.*
Practice Masters	Additional practice for every lesson in the Student Edition. *Also available as a workbook for Pre-Algebra.*
Study Guide and Practice Workbook	A consumable version of the Study Guide Masters and Practice Masters for each lesson. *Also available in Spanish.* (MAC 3 only)
Transition Booklet	Helps identify students weak in certain prerequisite skills. (MAC 3 only)
Parent and Student Study Guide Workbook	A review of every lesson that can be used by the parent and student. *Also available in Spanish.*
Spanish Study Guide and Assessment	Spanish translations of lesson objectives, Study Guide Masters, and free response Chapter Tests.

Technology Products	
MathPASS CD-ROM	Offers a complete, self-paced, easy-to-use interactive tutorial program for *Mathematics: Applications and Connections*, Course 3.
Pre-AlgePASS CD-ROM	Offers a complete, self-pace, easy-to-use interactive tutorial program for *Pre-Algebra*.
TestCheck and Worksheet Builder	Networkable software includes a Worksheet Builder to make worksheets and tests, a Student Module to take tests on-screen, and a Management System.
MindJogger Videoquizzes	Chapter review provided in a game-show format. *Available in VHS and DVD.*
Vocabulary PuzzleMaker Software	Improves students' mathematics vocabulary using crossword puzzles, scrambles, and word searches.
Glencoe Internet Site	Visit **glencoe.com** and find Online Study Tools, including self-grading lesson-by-lesson reviews, standardized test practice, and vocabulary review.

© Glencoe/McGraw-Hill — Diagnostic and Placement Tests

Placement Test 4 Diagnostic Chart

Placement Options:
Algebra 1: Concepts and Applications
or
Algebra 1
or
Algebra 1, Volumes One and Two

	Content	Suggestions for Intervention/Remediation
Part 1	Basic number concepts using fractions and decimals	These questions should be easy for beginning algebra students. If students score low, check to see whether they have made mistakes in marking their answers or in understanding the instructions. Students who score low may need additional help outside of algebra class.
Part 2	Pre-algebra concepts using graphic models	These questions should be easy for students with a visual learning style. They indicate whether students have mastered pre-algebra concepts at a concrete level. If students have difficulty here, they may need more work with hands-on, manipulative activities.
Part 3	Pre-algebra concepts using symbols	Students who find these questions challenging may benefit from activities using manipulatives and visual aids. They may need extra help in moving from the concrete to the abstract level of thinking.
Part 4	Two-step, verbal problems, basic algebra and function concepts, graphs	Questions 25 and 26 require reading and problem-solving skills. If students have difficulty, check their English language skill level. Question 27 combines rational number operations and positive exponents. Questions 28 and 29 require translations of mathematical words into symbols. Questions 30–33 require graphing skill. Questions 33 and 34 involve plotting points and graphing lines.

Intervention/Remediation Materials

Algebra 1: Integration, Applications, Connections
and
Algebra: Concepts and Applications

Print Materials

Study Guide Masters	A brief explanation, along with examples and exercises, for every lesson in the Student Edition. *Also available as a workbook.*
Practice Masters	Additional practice for every lesson in the Student Edition. *Also available as a workbook.*
Prerequisite Skills	Study guide and practice pages for each of 50 prerequisite skills that review algebra.
Parent and Student Study Guide Workbook	A review of every lesson that can be used by the parent and student. *Also available in Spanish.*
Spanish Study Guide and Assessment	Spanish translations of lesson objectives, Study Guide Masters, and free response Chapter Tests.

Technology Products

AlgePASS CD-ROM	Offers a complete, self-paced, easy-to-use interactive tutorial program.
TestCheck and Worksheet Builder	Networkable software includes a Worksheet Builder to make worksheets and tests, a Student Module to take tests on-screen, and a Management System to keep student records.
MindJogger Videoquizzes	Chapter review provided in a game-show format. *Available in VHS and DVD.*
Vocabulary PuzzleMaker Software	Improves students' mathematics vocabulary using crossword puzzles, scrambles, and word searches.
Glencoe Internet Site	Visit **glencoe.com** and find Online Study Tools, including self-grading lesson-by-lesson reviews, standardized test practice, and vocabulary review.

© Glencoe/McGraw-Hill — Diagnostic and Placement Tests

Diagnostic and Placement Test 1

Name _____

Date _____

This test contains 30 multiple-choice questions. Work each problem in the space on this page. Select the best answer. Write the letter of the answer on the blank at the right.

Part 1

1. Which set of numbers is in order from least to greatest?
   a. 721, 691, 522, 718, 709
   b. 522, 691, 718, 709, 721
   c. 522, 691, 709, 718, 721
   d. 721, 691, 522, 718, 709

   1. _____

2. What is 8,342 rounded to the nearest hundred?
   a. 8,340
   b. 8,300
   c. 8,400
   d. 8,000

   2. _____

3. 354 + 78 = __?__
   a. 322
   b. 332
   c. 422
   d. 432

   3. _____

4. 402 − 49 = __?__
   a. 353
   b. 363
   c. 451
   d. 453

   4. _____

5. A color printer can print six pages per minute. How long will it take to print 24 pages?
   a. 2.4 min
   b. 3 min
   c. 4 min
   d. 6 min

   5. _____

© Glencoe/McGraw-Hill

Diagnostic and Placement Tests

6. Two classes set a goal of collecting a total of 500 cans for the food drive. Mr. Hart's class collected 123 cans. Ms. Zani's class collected 237 cans. How many more cans are needed to reach the goal?
   a. 114
   b. 140
   c. 263
   d. 360

6. _____

Part 2

7. $8.4 - 3.73 = \underline{}$
   a. 3.11
   b. 4.67
   c. 4.77
   d. 5.1

7. _____

8. $6 \times 4.35 = \underline{}$
   a. 2.61
   b. 25.83
   c. 26.10
   d. 261.00

8. _____

9. Which is the simplest form for $\frac{8}{12}$?
   a. $\frac{1}{2}$
   b. $\frac{2}{3}$
   c. $\frac{4}{6}$
   d. $\frac{8}{12}$

9. _____

10. What is the least common denominator (LCD) of $\frac{3}{4}$ and $\frac{1}{6}$?
    a. 2
    b. 10
    c. 12
    d. 24

10. _____

11. Which decimal is equivalent to the fraction $\frac{7}{100}$?
    a. 0.007
    b. 0.07
    c. 0.7
    d. 7.0

11. _____

12. Which fraction is equivalent to 0.3?
    a. $\frac{0.3}{10}$
    b. $\frac{3}{100}$
    c. $\frac{3}{10}$
    d. $\frac{30}{10}$

12. _____

13. How many centimeters are there in 0.36 meters?
    a. 3.6
    b. 13
    c. 36
    d. 360

13. _____

14. What is the area of the rectangle below?
    a. 4 cm^2
    b. 15 cm^2
    c. 21 cm^2
    d. 36 cm^2

    3 cm
    12 cm

14. _____

15. Which number is greater than 0.7?
    a. 0.15
    b. 0.65
    c. 0.09
    d. 0.72

15. _____

16. Which decimal represents $\frac{3}{5}$?

    a. 0.03
    b. 0.3
    c. 0.06
    d. 0.6

16. _____

17. Keira was paid $2.50, $3.75, and $4 for baby-sitting on three evenings. What is the total amount she earned baby-sitting?

    a. $7.29
    b. $9.25
    c. $9.80
    d. $10.25

17. _____

18. Tom had an 8-foot piece of rope. He used $5\frac{1}{2}$ feet of rope to tie a young tree to a stake. How much rope was left over?

    a. $2\frac{1}{2}$ ft
    b. $3\frac{1}{2}$ ft
    c. $4\frac{1}{2}$ ft
    d. $5\frac{1}{2}$ ft

18. _____

(Part 3)

---

19. If $x = 10.05 - 2.4$, then $x = $ __?__

    a. 7.65
    b. 8.1
    c. 8.65
    d. 9.81

19. _____

20. If the British unit of money, the pound, is worth 1.45 dollars ($1.45), what is the value of 220 pounds?

    a. $31.90
    b. $319.00
    c. $580.00
    d. $3190.00

20. _____

21. Which fraction is expressed in simplest form?

    a. $\frac{2}{6}$

    b. $\frac{5}{8}$

    c. $\frac{3}{9}$

    d. $\frac{5}{15}$

21. _____

22. For which pair of fractions is the least common denominator (LCD) equal to one of the denominators?

    a. $\frac{1}{10}, \frac{1}{5}$

    b. $\frac{1}{2}, \frac{1}{3}$

    c. $\frac{1}{4}, \frac{1}{6}$

    d. $\frac{1}{10}, \frac{1}{8}$

22. _____

23. Which decimal is equivalent $10\frac{5}{100}$?

    a. 10.005

    b. 10.05

    c. 10.5

    d. 15

23. _____

24. Which number expresses 2.75 as a mixed number in simplest form?

    a. $2\frac{3}{4}$

    b. $2\frac{15}{20}$

    c. $2\frac{75}{100}$

    d. $2\frac{75}{10}$

24. _____

25. Jose is 173 centimeters tall. What is his height in meters?

    a. 0.0173 m

    b. 0.173 m

    c. 1.73 m

    d. 17.3 m

25. _____

26. What is the area of the figure below? 26. _____
   a. 24 in²
   b. 46 in²
   c. 56 in²
   d. 640 in²   4 in.   8 in.
                  ← 10 in. →
                          2 in.

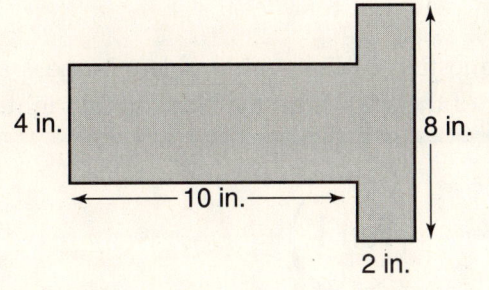

27. Which list of decimals is in order from least to greatest? 27. _____
   a. 0.1, 0.14, 0.05, 0.08, 0.32
   b. 0.1, 0.05, 0.08, 0.14, 0.32
   c. 0.1, 0.05, 0.08, 0.14, 0.32
   d. 0.05, 0.08, 0.1, 0.14, 0.32

28. Which number represents one hundred three and eighteen thousandths? 28. _____
   a. 130.18
   b. 103.18
   c. 103.018
   d. 103.0018

29. Sara bought a paperback book for $7.79. She gave the clerk a $10 bill. About how much change should she get? 29. _____
   a. $1
   b. $2
   c. $3
   d. $4

30. Rene is making a border across the top of a bulletin board that is 51 inches long. She uses pieces of red paper that are $8\frac{1}{2}$ inches long, placed end to end. How many pieces of paper will she need? 30. _____
   a. 4
   b. 6
   c. $42\frac{1}{2}$
   d. $59\frac{1}{2}$

© Glencoe/McGraw-Hill   Diagnostic and Placement Tests

Diagnostic and Placement Test 2

Name _____

Date _____

This test contains 30 multiple-choice questions. Work each problem in the space on this page. Select the best answer. Write the letter of the answer on the blank at the right.

Part 1

1. $7.6 - 5.88 = \underline{}$
   a. 1.72
   b. 1.82
   c. 2.72
   d. 2.88

   1. _____

2. $3.84 \times 5 = \underline{}$
   a. 1.92
   b. 15.42
   c. 19.20
   d. 192.00

   2. _____

3. Which is the simplest form of $\frac{6}{24}$?
   a. $\frac{3}{12}$
   b. $\frac{2}{8}$
   c. $\frac{1}{4}$
   d. $\frac{1}{2}$

   3. _____

4. What is the least common denominator (LCD) of $\frac{7}{10}$ and $\frac{5}{6}$?
   a. 2
   b. 16
   c. 30
   d. 60

   4. _____

5. Which decimal is equivalent to the fraction $\frac{80}{1,000}$?
   a. 0.008
   b. 0.080
   c. 0.800
   d. 8.000

   5. _____

© Glencoe/McGraw-Hill

Diagnostic and Placement Tests

6. Which fraction is equivalent to 0.07?
   a. $\frac{0.7}{100}$
   b. $\frac{7}{1,000}$
   c. $\frac{7}{100}$
   d. $\frac{70}{10}$

6. _____

7. Which number is less than 0.08?
   a. 0.7
   b. 0.16
   c. 0.083
   d. 0.075

7. _____

8. Which decimal represents $1\frac{5}{8}$?
   a. 0.625
   b. 1.4
   c. 1.625
   d. 1.6

8. _____

9. A bamboo plant can grow 35.4 inches per day. About how many inches can it grow in an hour?
   a. 0.7
   b. 1.5
   c. 3
   d. 11.4

9. _____

10. What is the area of a rectangular field with width $\frac{1}{2}$ mile and length $\frac{5}{8}$ mile?
    a. $\frac{5}{16}$ sq mi
    b. $\frac{1}{2}$ sq mi
    c. $\frac{3}{5}$ sq mi
    d. $\frac{9}{8}$ sq mi

10. _____

Part 2

11. Which fraction is equivalent to $\frac{2}{5}$?

    a. $\frac{7}{10}$

    b. $\frac{12}{15}$

    c. $\frac{5}{25}$

    d. $\frac{12}{30}$

11. _____

12. Which statement is true?

    a. $\frac{1}{2} < \frac{1}{4}$

    b. $\frac{1}{3} > \frac{5}{6}$

    c. $\frac{3}{4} > \frac{1}{3}$

    d. $\frac{2}{3} < \frac{1}{5}$

12. _____

13. $5 + 3 \cdot 8 = $ __?__

    a. 16

    b. 19

    c. 29

    d. 64

13. _____

14. Which decimal has the same value as $\frac{7}{20}$?

    a. 0.035

    b. 0.07

    c. 0.28

    d. 0.35

14. _____

15. $23.15 \cdot 100 = $ __?__

    a. 0.2315

    b. 2.315

    c. 231.5

    d. 2,315

15. _____

16. Which statement shows the commutative property of multiplication?
   a. $5 \times \frac{1}{5} = 1$
   b. $5 \times 3 = 3 \times 5$
   c. $5 \times (3 \times 2) = (5 \times 193) \times 2$
   d. $5(3 + 2) = 5 \times 3 + 5 \times 2$

16. _____

17. For the integer marked *P* on the number line, what is its opposite?
   a. −4
   b. 0
   c. 1
   d. 4

17. _____

18. If $x = 3$ and $y = 2$, then $2x - y = \underline{\ ?\ }$.
   a. 1
   b. 2
   c. 3
   d. 4

18. _____

19. How much fencing will be needed to fence the garden in the diagram below?
   a. $23\frac{3}{4}$ ft
   b. $29\frac{1}{4}$ ft
   c. $47\frac{1}{2}$ ft
   d. $58\frac{1}{2}$ ft

   $5\frac{1}{2}$ ft
   $18\frac{1}{4}$ ft

19. _____

20. What is the area of the triangle below? The area of a triangle is expressed by the formula $A = \frac{1}{2}bh$.
   a. 270 cm²
   b. 288 cm²
   c. 480 cm²
   d. 540 cm²

   18 cm
   30 cm
   32 cm

20. _____

© Glencoe/McGraw-Hill — Diagnostic and Placement Tests

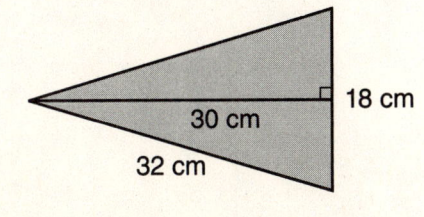

Part 3

21. Which list contains three equivalent fractions?
    a. $\frac{1}{2}, \frac{3}{8}, \frac{7}{12}$
    b. $\frac{2}{3}, \frac{16}{24}, \frac{6}{9}$
    c. $\frac{1}{3}, \frac{3}{12}, \frac{11}{30}$
    d. $\frac{1}{4}, \frac{2}{8}, \frac{5}{10}$

21. _____

22. Which number is closest to 2?
    a. $2\frac{6}{15}$
    b. $1\frac{4}{5}$
    c. $2\frac{3}{5}$
    d. $1\frac{14}{15}$

22. _____

23. $3(4 + 6) \div 6 = $ __?__
    a. 3
    b. 5
    c. 10
    d. 12

23. _____

24. Which percent is equivalent to $\frac{8}{25}$?
    a. 8%
    b. 12%
    c. 32%
    d. 80%

24. _____

25. $6.74 \times 10^3 = $ __?__
    a. 67.4
    b. 674
    c. 6,740
    d. 67,400

25. _____

26. Which expression is equivalent to 1.5 × (2.2 × 3.9)?
    a. (1.5 × 2.2) + (2.2 × 3.9)
    b. 1.5 × (2.2 + 3.9)
    c. 1.5 + (2.2 × 3.9)
    d. (1.5 × 2.2) × 3.9

26. _____

27. For the integer marked N on the number line, which set lists the integer, its opposite, and its absolute value in order?
    a. {−3, 3, −3}
    b. {−3, 3, 3}
    c. {−3, −3, 3}
    d. {3, −3, 3}

27. _____

28. If $r = 4$, $s = 7$, and $t = 2$ then $\frac{t(r+s)-s}{r+1} = \underline{\ ?\ }$.
    a. $\frac{8}{5}$
    b. 3
    c. 15
    d. 22

28. _____

29. Which has the greater perimeter, a square with side 8 units or a rectangle with length 14 units and width 2 units?
    a. the square
    b. the rectangle
    c. the perimeters are equal
    d. It cannot be determined.

29. _____

30. You want to build a deck in the shape of a trapezoid. The bases are to be 10 feet and 14 feet, and the area must be 120 square feet. What is the height? (The formula for the area of a trapezoid is $A = \frac{1}{2}h(a+b)$.)
    a. 5 ft
    b. 10 ft
    c. 12 ft
    d. 30 ft

30. _____

© Glencoe/McGraw-Hill

Diagnostic and Placement Tests

Diagnostic and Placement Test 3

Name _____

Date _____

This test contains 30 multiple-choice questions. Work each problem in the space on this page. Select the best answer. Write the letter of the answer on the blank at the right.

Part 1

1. Which fraction is NOT equivalent to $\frac{3}{20}$?
   a. $\frac{35}{100}$
   b. $\frac{28}{80}$
   c. $\frac{21}{60}$
   d. $\frac{14}{50}$

1. _____

2. Which fraction is less than $\frac{3}{4}$?
   a. $\frac{7}{8}$
   b. $\frac{7}{12}$
   c. $\frac{15}{16}$
   d. $\frac{17}{20}$

2. _____

3. Evaluate $\frac{t^2 - s \cdot 8 \div 2}{s + 5}$ when $s = 3$ and $t = 4$.
   a. -10
   b. $\frac{1}{2}$
   c. $\frac{14}{5}$
   d. $\frac{13}{2}$

3. _____

4. Which decimal has the same value as $\frac{7}{8}$?
   a. 0.75
   b. 0.777
   c. 0.875
   d. 0.975

4. _____

© Glencoe/McGraw-Hill

5. Express 5% as a fraction in simplest form.   5. _____
   a. $\frac{1}{5}$
   b. $\frac{1}{20}$
   c. $\frac{5}{100}$
   d. $\frac{20}{100}$

6. $8.2 \times 10^3 =$ __?__   6. _____
   a. 82
   b. 820
   c. 8,200
   d. 82,000

7. Which statement shows the associative property of multiplication?   7. _____
   a. $4 \times \frac{1}{4} = 1$
   b. $4 \times 3 = 3 \times 4$
   c. $4 \times (3 \times 7) = (4 \times 3) \times 7$
   d. $4(3 + 7) = 4 \times 3 + 4 \times 7$

8. What is the perimeter of a rectangle with length 16.8 units and width 9.6 units?   8. _____
   a. 26.4
   b. 43.2
   c. 52.8
   d. 161.28

9. What is the area of a triangle with base $3\frac{1}{2}$ feet and height 6 feet? (The formula for the area of a triangle is $A = \frac{1}{2}bh$.)   9. _____
   a. $4\frac{1}{2}$ ft²
   b. $4\frac{3}{4}$ ft²
   c. $10\frac{1}{2}$ ft²
   d. 21 ft²

10. What is the area of a trapezoid with height 8 centimeters and bases 3.6 centimeters and 11.8 centimeters? (The formula for the area of a trapezoid is $A = \frac{1}{2}h(a + b)$.)   10. _____
    a. 22.68 cm²
    b. 61.8 cm²
    c. 68.44 cm²
    d. 123.6 cm²

© Glencoe/McGraw-Hill   Diagnostic and Placement Tests

Part 2

11. What is the decimal representation for the fraction $\frac{1}{3}$?   11. _____
    a. 0.3
    b. 0.30
    c. $0.\overline{3}$
    d. 0.33

12. $5\left(\frac{1}{5} - x\right) = \underline{\quad ?\quad}$ 12. _____
    a. $5 - x$
    b. $1 - 5x$
    c. $1 + 5x$
    d. $1 - x$

13. Solve the proportion for w. $\frac{2}{3} = \frac{5}{w}$ 13. _____
    a. 1.2
    b. 3.3
    c. 4
    d. 7.5.

14. Solve the equation $k = -\frac{3}{4} + \frac{5}{8}$.   14. _____
    a. $-\frac{30}{8}$
    b. $-\frac{11}{8}$
    c. $-\frac{1}{8}$
    d. $\frac{11}{8}$

15. Solve the equation $t = 4\frac{1}{2} \div \frac{3}{4}$.   15. _____
    a. $\frac{8}{3}$
    b. $\frac{27}{8}$
    c. 5
    d. 6

16. In a factory, a worker assembles 20 CD players in 8 hours. Express the ratio as a unit rate.

    a. 0.4 players per hour
    b. 1.5 players per hour
    c. 2.5 players per hour
    d. 4 players per hour

16. _____

17. 40 is what percent of 500?

    a. 1.25%
    b. 8%
    c. 12.5%
    d. 80%

17. _____

18. What is the next term in the sequence $-13, -9, -5, -1, \ldots$?

    a. -4
    b. -3
    c. 3
    d. 4

18. _____

19. Which expression represents the height of the Gateway Arch in St. Louis if it is 75 feet taller than the Washington Monument, which is represented by w?

    a. $w - 75$
    b. $w + 75$
    c. $75w$
    d. $75 - w$

19. _____

20. Jed walks at a steady pace. Then he runs down a hill. Which graph best represents his speed versus his time?

    a. 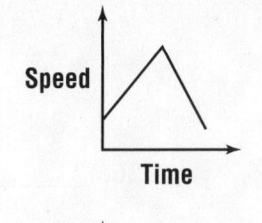
    b. 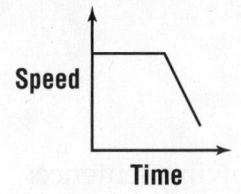
    c. 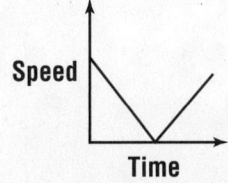
    d.

20. _____

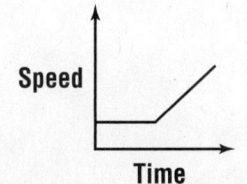

Part 3

21. Which fraction is equivalent to a repeating decimal?

    a. $\frac{1}{2}$ **b.** $\frac{1}{5}$

    c. $\frac{1}{6}$ **d.** $\frac{1}{8}$

21. _____

22. Solve the equation $4(x + 2) = 34$.

    a. $6\frac{1}{2}$

    b. 8

    c. 9

    d. $10\frac{1}{2}$

22. _____

23. If n is a positive integer and t is a fraction between 0 and 1, which is greater, nt or $\frac{n}{t}$?

    a. nt is greater

    b. $\frac{n}{t}$ is greater

    c. they are equal

    d. It cannot be determined.

23. _____

24. Solve the equation $\frac{s}{3} - 5 = -14$.

    a. -57 **b.** -27

    c. 9   **d.** 27

24. _____

25. What is the next term in the sequence $-3, 1, -\frac{1}{3}, \frac{1}{9}, \ldots$?

    a. $-\frac{1}{27}$ **b.** $-\frac{1}{3}$

    c. $\frac{1}{27}$ **d.** $\frac{1}{3}$

25. _____

26. Which equation represents the following sentence: The product of w and 12 is 84.

    a. $\frac{w}{12} = 84$

    b. $w + 12 = 84$

    c. $w = 12(84)$

    d. $12w = 84$

26. _____

27. Which pair of numbers are equal?

    a. 1^2 and 2^1
    b. 3^2 and 2^3
    c. 4^2 and 2^4
    d. 5^2 and 2^5

27. _____

28. The points (2, −3), (8, 3), and (2, 3) are three of the vertices of a square. What are the coordinates of the fourth vertex?

    a. (−8, −3)
    b. (−8, 3)
    c. (−2, 3)
    d. (8, −3)

28. _____

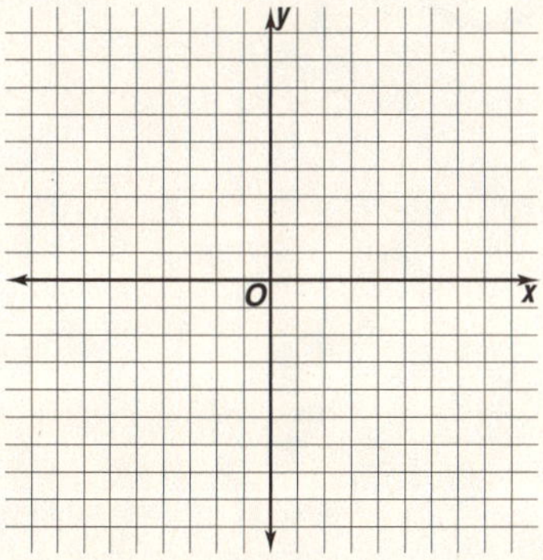

29. The stem-and-leaf plot below shows the ages of the workers at the Generations Internet Company. What is the median age of a typical worker?

    a. 18
    b. 25
    c. 35
    d. 67

Stem	Leaf
1	8 9 9
2	0 0 1 2 2 3 3 4 5 5 7
3	5 7
4	2 9
5	5 6 6
6	6 7 7 7

6 | 7 = 67

29. _____

30. Which is the most appropriate graph for this data table?

Immigration into the United States

Year	1988	1989	1990	1991	1992	1993
Immigrants (millions)	0.6	1.1	1.5	1.8	1.0	0.9

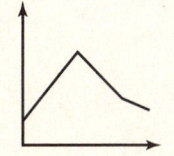

a.

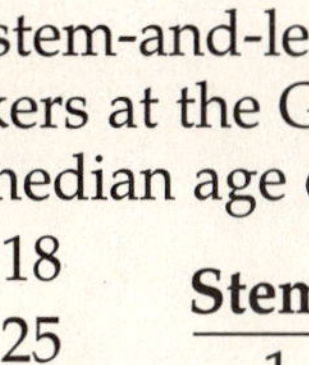

b.

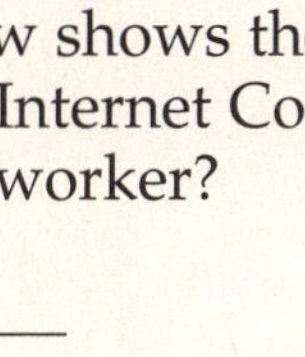

c.

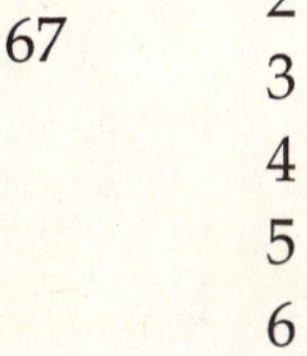

d.

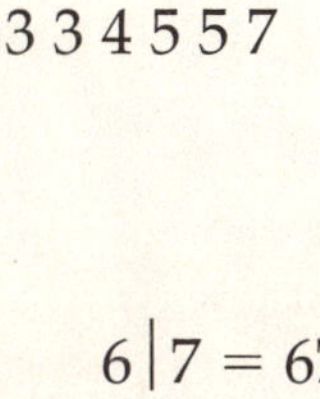

30. _____

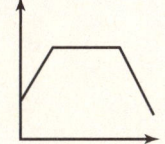

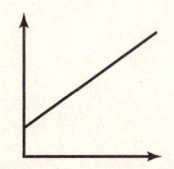

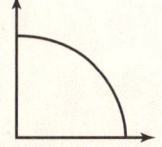

Diagnostic and Placement Test 4

Name _____

Date _____

This test contains 32 multiple-choice questions. Work each problem in the space on this page. Select the best answer. Write the letter of the answer on the blank at the right.

Part 1

1. $\frac{3}{8} \cdot \frac{4}{9} = \underline{\ ?\ }$
   a. $\frac{1}{6}$
   b. $\frac{1}{5}$
   c. $\frac{1}{3}$
   d. $\frac{7}{17}$

   1. _____

2. $\frac{5}{4} - \frac{5}{6} = \underline{\ ?\ }$
   a. 0
   b. $\frac{5}{24}$
   c. $\frac{5}{12}$
   d. $\frac{25}{12}$

   2. _____

3. What is the decimal representation for $\frac{3}{8}$?
   a. 0.037
   b. 0.3
   c. 0.375
   d. 0.38

   3. _____

4. $3\frac{3}{4} \div 2\frac{1}{2} = \underline{\ ?\ }$
   a. $\frac{2}{3}$
   b. $\frac{3}{2}$
   c. $\frac{25}{4}$
   d. $\frac{25}{3}$

   4. _____

5. $3(5 + x) = \underline{\ ?\ }$
   a. $8 + x$
   b. $15 + x$
   c. $15x$
   d. $15 + 3x$

   5. _____

© Glencoe/McGraw-Hill

6. Solve the proportion for n. $\frac{5}{4} = \frac{n}{12}$

    a. $\frac{17}{4}$

    b. $\frac{48}{5}$

    c. 15

    d. 60

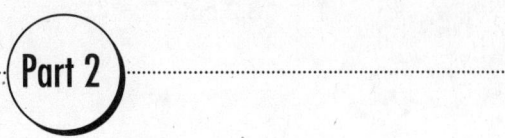

6. _____

Part 2

7. Use the number line to solve $-5 + 3$.

    a. -8

    b. -2

    c. 2

    d. 8

7. _____

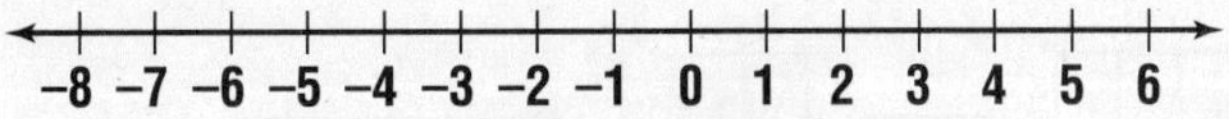

8. Use the counters pictured below to solve the equation $2x + 5 = 9$.

    a. 2

    b. 4

    c. 7

    d. 8

8. _____

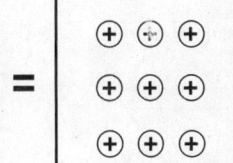

9. What are the coordinates of the point labeled P?

    a. $(-5, -5)$

    b. $(-3, -5)$

    c. $(-5, 3)$

    d. $(-3, 5)$

9. _____

© Glencoe/McGraw-Hill   Diagnostic and Placement Tests

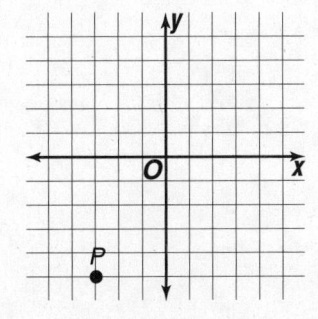

10. What is the area of the trapezoid below with height 6 centimeters and bases 3.2 centimeters and 7.4 centimeters? (The formula for the area of a trapezoid is $A = \frac{1}{2}h(a + b)$.)
    a. 21.44 cm²
    b. 31.8 cm²
    c. 34.04 cm²
    d. 63.44 cm²

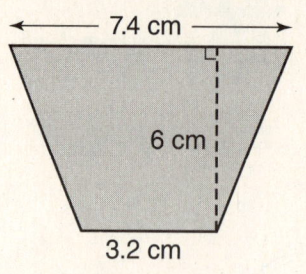

10. _____

11. Use the algebra tiles below to simplify the polynomial expression $5x - 2 - 3x + 5$.
    a. $2x - 3$
    b. $2x + 3$
    c. $8x + 3$
    d. $8x + 7$

11. _____

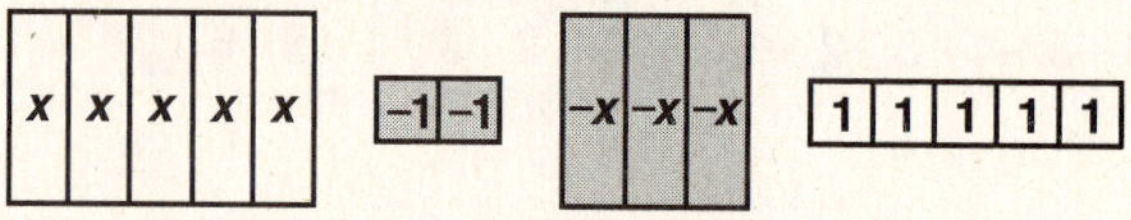

12. What is the area of the parallelogram below?
    a. 16 in²
    b. 20 in²
    c. 32 in²
    d. 40 in²

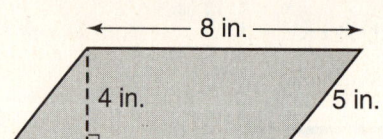

12. _____

(Part 3)

13. What is the next term in the sequence 7, 1, −5, −11 . . . ?
    a. −17
    b. −15
    c. 5
    d. 17

13. _____

14. $(-4)(-2)(-3) = $ __?__
    a. -24
    b. -11
    c. 5
    d. 24

14. _____

15. $-18 - (-6) = $ __?__
    a. -24
    b. -12
    c. 12
    d. 24

15. _____

16. Evaluate $\frac{v^2 - 4 \cdot v - 2}{t + 2}$ when $t = 3$ and $v = 5$.
    a. -17
    b. $\frac{3}{5}$
    c. $\frac{18}{5}$
    d. 9

16. _____

17. Express the number 0.0047 in scientific notation.
    a. 4.7×10^3
    b. 4.7×10^{-4}
    c. 4.7×10^{-3}
    d. 4.7×10^{-2}

17. _____

18. Express the ratio 6 inches of rain in 24 hours as a unit rate.
    a. $\frac{1}{6}$ inch per hour
    b. $\frac{1}{4}$ inch per hour
    c. $2\frac{1}{2}$ inches per hour
    d. 4 inches per hour

18. _____

© Glencoe/McGraw-Hill   Diagnostic and Placement Tests

19. Express $\frac{5}{8}$ as a percent.	19. _____
   a. 0.625%	b. 6.25%
   c. 62.5%	d. 625%

20. 15 is 30% of what number? Use the percent equation, $P = RB$, where P is the percentage, R is the rate, and B is the base.	20. _____
   a. 0.5	b. 4.5
   c. 45	d. 50

21. Solve the equation $4x - 5 = 7$.	21. _____
   a. $\frac{1}{2}$
   b. 3
   c. 8
   d. 12

22. This is a function table for $f(n) = 2n - 1$. What is the missing value?	22. _____

n	$2n - 1$	$f(n)$
0	2(0) − 1	−1
1	2(1) − 1	1
2	2(2) − 1	3
3	2(3) − 1	

   a. −3
   b. 4
   c. 5
   d. 6

Part 4

23. Colin has $15.00 to spend. He wants to rent a video for $4.50 and buy a pack of soda for $5.00 and chips for $2.50. How much money will he have left?	23. _____
   a. $3	b. $4
   c. $11	d. $12

24. The Schmidt family will make a 1080 mile round trip on their vacation. Their car gets about 20 miles per gallon of gasoline. Gasoline costs about $1.50 per gallon. How much will the gasoline cost for their trip?
    a. $30
    b. $36
    c. $54
    d. $81

24. _____

25. Evaluate $\left(\dfrac{-3}{5}\right)^2$.
    a. $\dfrac{-9}{25}$
    b. $\dfrac{6}{25}$
    c. $\dfrac{9}{25}$
    d. $\dfrac{9}{5}$

25. _____

26. Which set contains integers that are less than -1 and greater than -6?
    a. $\{-7, -6, -5, -3\}$
    b. $\{-5, -4, -2, 0\}$
    c. $\{-4, -3, -2, -1\}$
    d. $\{-5, -4, -3, -2\}$

26. _____

27. Which algebraic expression matches the verbal expression, "the amount of money in Tad's account if he starts with s dollars and adds d dollars each week for 12 weeks"?
    a. $12s + d$
    b. $s + 12d$
    c. $12(s + d)$
    d. $12ds$

27. _____

28. Which data set would create a scatter plot like the one shown below?

    a. height and month of birth
    b. hours you train for a race and time you take to finish a race
    c. number of people in a household and weekly food cost
    d. temperature and day of the week

28. _____

29. Kristin walks at a steady pace. Then she runs down a hill. Which graph best represents her speed versus her time?

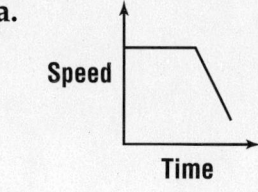

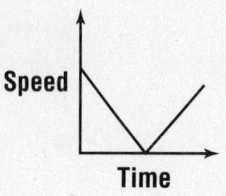

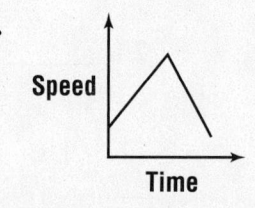

a. [Speed vs Time graph: flat then decreasing]
b. [Speed vs Time graph: decreasing to zero then increasing]
c. [Speed vs Time graph: increasing then decreasing]
d. [Speed vs Time graph: flat then increasing]

29. _____

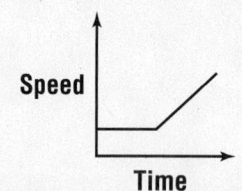

30. On the graph below, the solid line shows Company A's profits. The dashed line shows Company B's profits. In what year are Company A's profits greater than Company B's?

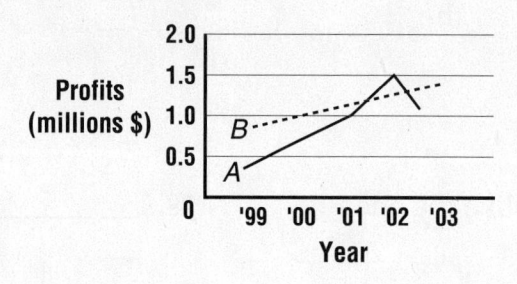

a. 1999
b. 2000
c. 2001
d. 2002

30. _____

31. Which set of ordered pairs represent points on the line that is graphed below?

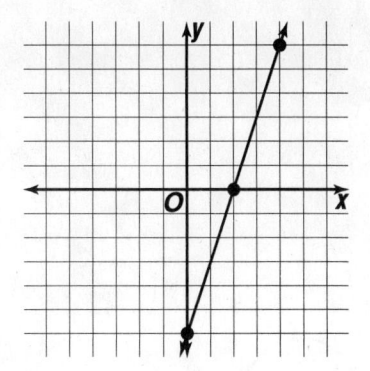

31. _____

a. (0, −6), (0, 2), (6, 4)
b. (0, −6), (2, 0), (4, 6)
c. (−6, 0), (0, 2), (4, 6)
d. (0, 6), (2, 0), (6, 4)

32. Which two ordered pairs are both solutions to the equation $y = -2x - 3$?
   a. (0, −3), (1, 5)
   b. (2, −1), (−1, −1)
   c. (2, −7), (1, 5)
   d. (0, −3), (1, −5)

32. _____

Placement Test 1 – Answer Key

Part 1

1. c
2. b
3. d
4. a
5. c

Part 2

6. b
7. b
8. c
9. b
10. c
11. b
12. c
13. c
14. d
15. d

Placement Test 1 – Answer Key

16. d
17. d
18. a

Part 3

19. a
20. b

21. b
22. a
23. b
24. a
25. c

26. c
27. d
28. c
29. b
30. b

Placement Test 2 – Answer Key

Part 1

1. a
2. c
3. c
4. c
5. b
6. c
7. d
8. c
9. b
10. a

Part 2

11. d
12. c
13. c
14. d
15. d

Placement Test 2 – Answer Key

16. b

17. a

18. d

19. c

20. a

Part 3

21. b

22. d

23. b

24. c

25. c

26. d

27. b

28. b

29. c

30. b

Placement Test 3 – Answer Key

Part 1

1. d
2. b
3. b
4. c
5. b
6. c
7. c
8. c
9. c
10. b

Part 2

11. c
12. b
13. d
14. c
15. d

Placement Test 3 – Answer Key

16. c

17. b

18. c

19. b

20. d

Part 3

21. c

22. a

23. b

24. b

25. a

26. d

27. c

28. d

29. b

30. a

Placement Test 4 – Answer Key

Part 1

1. a
2. c
3. c
4. b
5. d

Part 2

6. c
7. b
8. a
9. b
10. b
11. c
12. c
13. a

Part 3

14. a
15. b
16. b
17. c
18. b

Placement Test 4 – Answer Key

19. c
20. d
21. b
22. c
23. a

24. d
25. c
26. d
27. b
28. c

29. d
30. d

31. b
32. d

(Part 4)